Mel Bay Presents

Mastering the Guitar

A COMPREHENSIVE METHOD FOR TODAY'S GUITARIST!

2B

B356

By William Bay &
Mike Christiansen

William Bay

Mike Christiansen

Introduction

Mastering the Guitar is an innovative, comprehensive new method for learning the guitar. Special features in Level 2, Book A are the introduction of the new **Zone Concept** for learning position playing, the inclusion of more than 150 solos and duets in the keys of C, G, D, and B minor and the presentation of guitar solo literature in a colorful variety of styles (jazz, swing, Bossa Nova, be-bop, blues, ragtime, fiddle tunes, baroque, etc.).

...Several new approaches in this volume in...riation, ...ord pro-...ped-D ...breaks, ...rd stud-...perfor-...d rock comping.

Finally, guitar literature is included by composers such as J. S. Bach, Carcassi, Giuliani, Carulli, Vivaldi, Handel, Sor, Tarrega, Debussy, Corelli, and others. A companion double CD is available for this text and is highly recommended.

A recording of the music in this book is now available. The publisher strongly recommends the use of this recording along with the text to insure accuracy of interpretation and ease in learning.

Visit us on the Web at http://www.melbay.com — E-mail us at email@melbay.com

Zone I

Zone I

In Zone I, the 1st Finger of the Left Hand will always be between the First and Third frets.

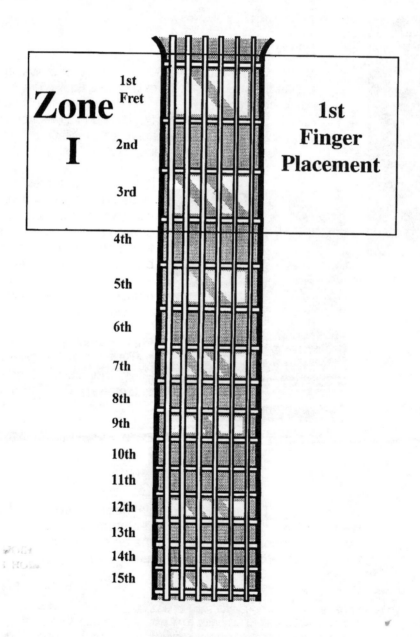

Key of A / Closed Position

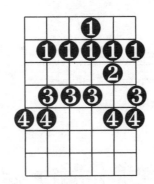

A Scale

Velocity Study #1

WB

Velocity Study #2

WB

Key of A

Velocity Study #3

WB

Velocity Study #4

WB

Key of A

London Hornpipe

CD #1
Track #1

Flatpick Solo

WB

Allegro ♩ = 78

CD #1
Track #2

Apollo Club Hornpipe

Flatpick Solo

WB

Lively ♩ = 76

NOTE: On the companion recording not all repeats are played.

Key of A

CD #1
Track #3

Shannon's Well

Flatpick Solo

WB

CD #1
Track #4

Chicago Slide

Flatpick Solo

WB

Key of A

Smuggler's Reel

Flatpick Solo

WB

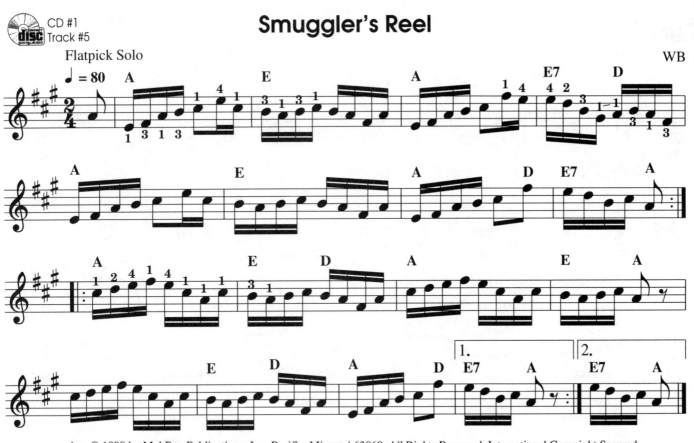

Crazy Creek

Flatpick Solo

WB

Key of A

CD #1
Track #7

Levee Rag

Flatpick Solo

Ragtime feeling ♩ = 150

WB

CD #1
Track #8

Fingers Galore

Flatpick Solo

♩ = 140

WB

Miss Johnson's Hornpipe

CD #1
Track #9

Flatpick Solo

WB

Arr. © 1999 by Mel Bay Publications, Inc. Pacific, Missouri 63069. All Rights Reserved. International Copyright Secured.

CD #1
Track #10

Bill Cheathum

Flatpick Solo

WB

Arr. © 1999 by Mel Bay Publications, Inc. Pacific, Missouri 63069. All Rights Reserved. International Copyright Secured.

Etude

WB
Clodmir

Torch Song

CD #1
Track #12

Slow ballad, with a beat

WB

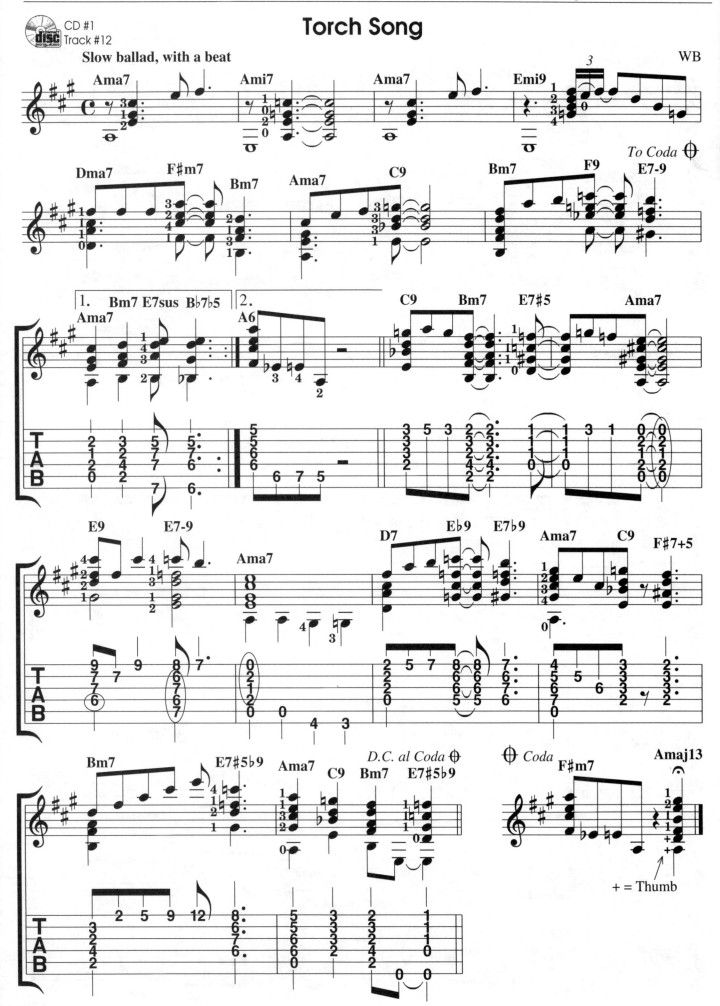

Key of A

The Promenade

CD #1
Track #16

Flatpick Solo

WB

Palermo Hornpipe

CD #1
Track #17

Flatpick Solo

WB

Duet in A

Gigue
From Sonata No. 9, Op. 5

Corelli

CD #1
Track #18

Key of A

Hills of Ireland

Flatpick Solo

♩. = 108

New Dawn

Flatpick Solo

Rock feeling ♩ = 140

Chords in the Key of A

I	ii	iii	IV	V	vi	VIIo
A	Bm	C#m	D	E7	F#m	G#dim

Drawn below are the chords in the key of A. The basic chords are shown first followed by embellishments and optional fingerings. Bm, F#m, and their embellishments are in the key of A, but they are not drawn below because they have been presented earlier.

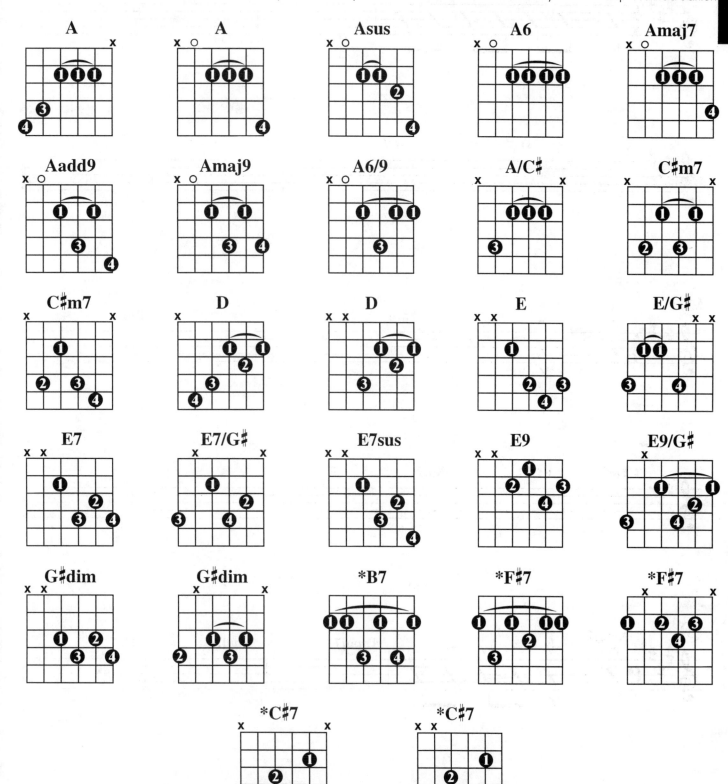

These chords are not actually in the key of A, but they are often used when playing music in A.

Chord Progressions in A

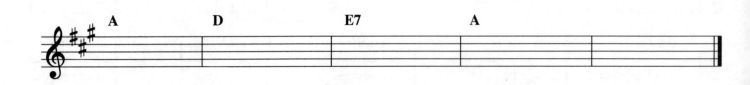

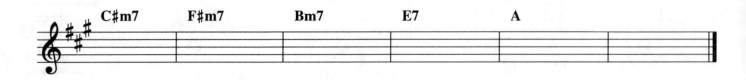

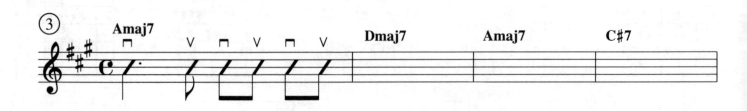

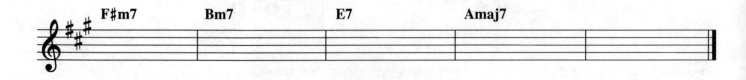

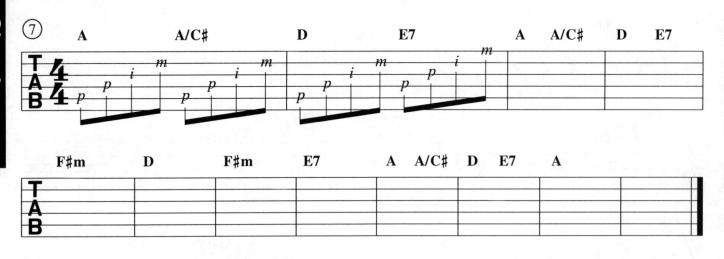

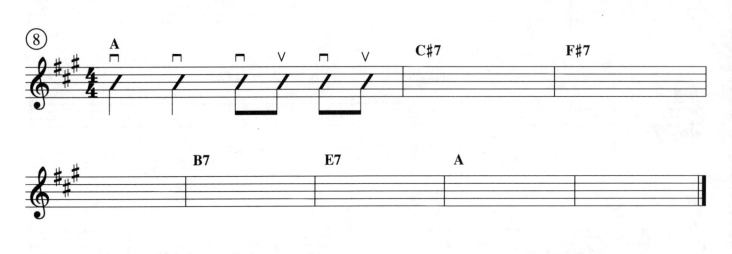

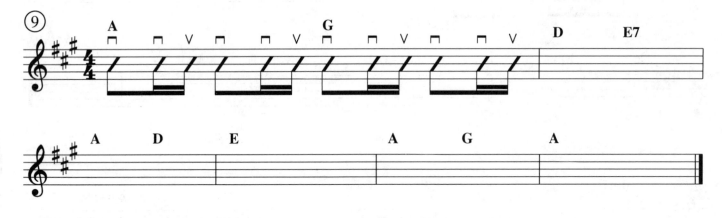

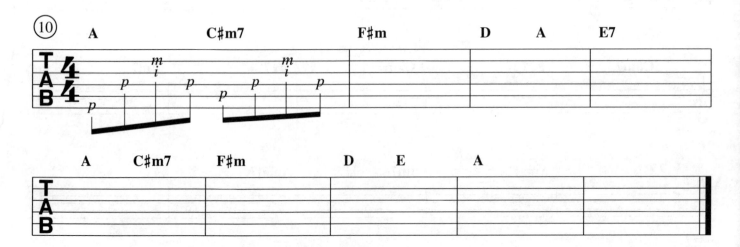

Chord Studies in the Key of A

Blues in A

Blues Progressions in A

Turnarounds in A

Blues in A

CD #1
Track #21

Blue Bop

Flatpick Solo

♩ = 100 (♫ = ♪♪♪)

MC

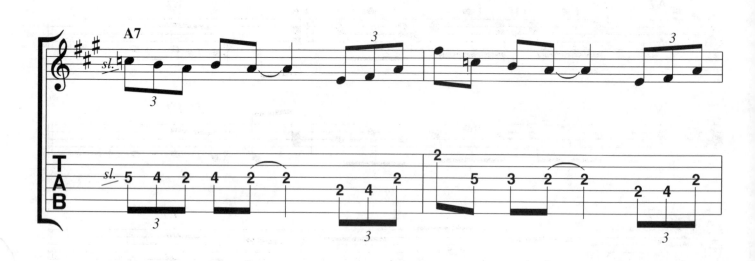

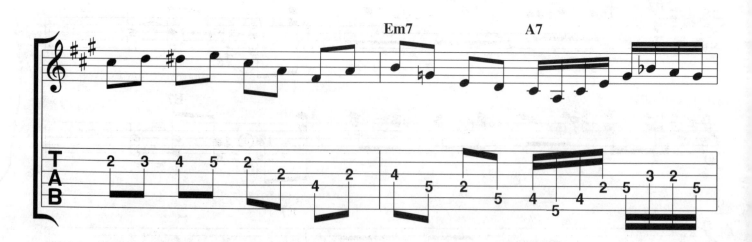

Blues in A

Licks/Fills/Breaks

Licks, Fills, and Breaks in the Key of A

Bending the Rules

CD #1
Track #22

MC

Basic Improvisation in A

Basic Chords and Arpeggios in the Key of A

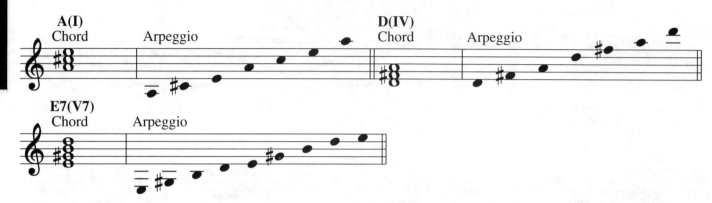

Play the following with a Jazz or Swing feeling

Basic Arpeggios

Passing Tone Arpeggio Study #1

Passing Tone Study #2

Chords/Arpeggios

Passing Tone Study #3

WB

Rhythmic Variation Study #1

WB

Rhythmic Variation Study #2

WB

Rhythmic Variation Study #3

WB

A Major Scale Harmonized

Summer Sunset

MC

Fingerstyle Solo

♩ = 76

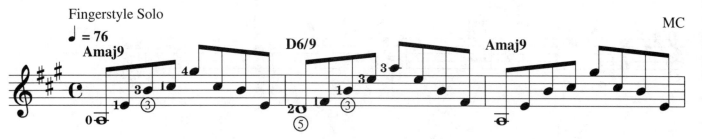

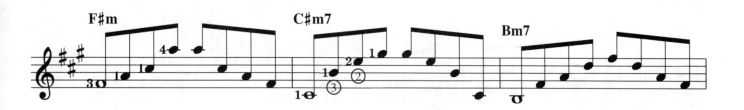

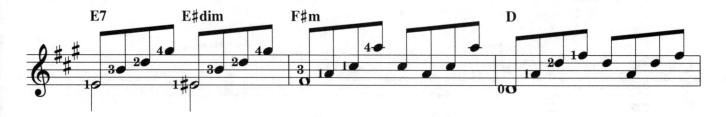

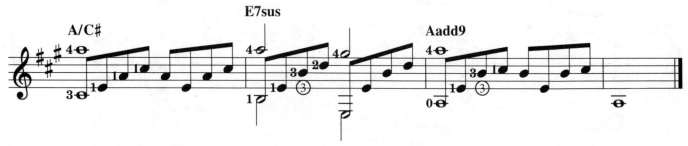

Fingerstyle Solos in A

CD #1
Track #24

Nuance

Fingerstyle
Easy jazz feeling ♩ = 116

WB

CD #1
Track #25

Images

Fingerstyle

WB

Slowly ♩ = 68

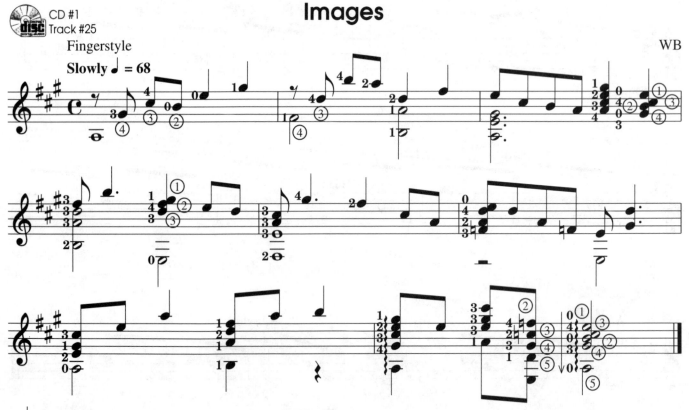

* ↓ means to strum down from the high strings to the low strings.

CD #1
Track #26

Hangin' 'Round

Fingerstyle Solo

MC

Fingerstyle Solos in A

Etude

CD #1
Track #27

Fingerstyle

Andante ♩ = 44

WB
Sor

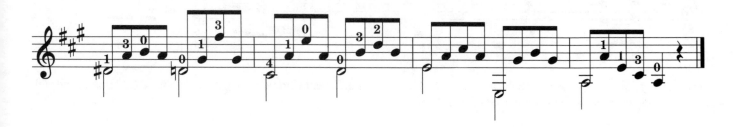

CD #1
Track #28

Barcarolle

WB
Napolean Coste

Fingerstyle Solo

Andante ♩ = 74

Harm. 12 *

* To play this harmonic — lightly touch the E string at the 12th fret — right over the fretwire — with the left hand (3rd finger) and at the same time pluck the string with the right hand index finger.

Prelude

CD #1
Track #29

Fingerstyle Solo
Freely, with expression
Andante ♩ = 80

WB
Weiss

Fingerstyle
Solos in A

Estudio 22

CD #1
Track #30

Fingerstyle Solo

MC

D. Aguado

Adagio ♩ = 66

Fingerstyle Solos in A

Fingerpicking Blues And Ragtime

Fingerpicking Blues/Ragtime

This section of the book contains fingerpicking blues solos. These solos are written in two different styles: those which have a steady bass, and those which have an alternating bass. In these fingerpicking styles, the right thumb plays the bass notes (strings 6, 5, and 4), and the right-hand fingers play the melody (usually on strings 1, 2, and 3).

In a "steady-bass" style, the thumb plays the same bass note (which has the same name as the chord for that measure) on each beat of the measure. The fingers play at the same time, or between the thumb strokes. This style of soloing was commonly used by early blues guitarists.

The following exercise will help prepare you to play the solos which have a steady bass. In all of the solos in this section of the book, the notes (or numbers) written with the stems going down are to be played with the thumb. The notes (or numbers) written with the stems going up are to be played with the fingers (generally, the first and second fingers of the right hand). The choice of which finger to use is up to you. Do not use the little finger.

All of the notes in the following exercise are played with the right-hand thumb.

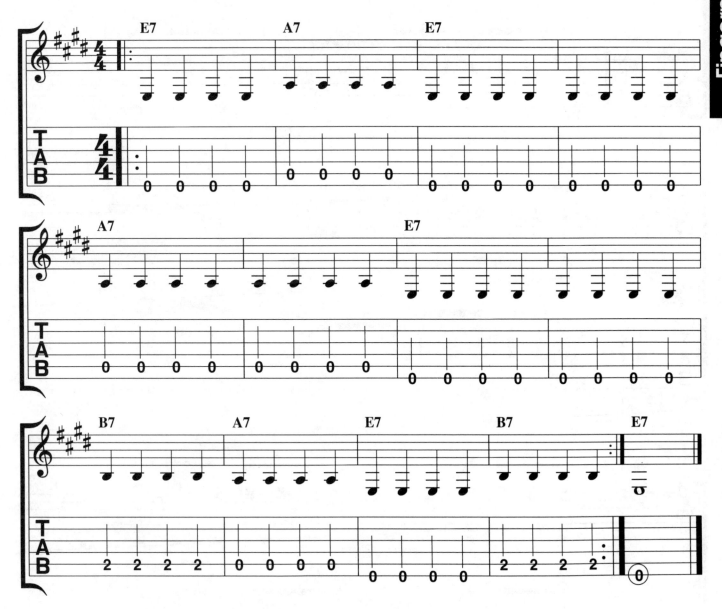

Unless otherwise indicated, all of the fingerpicking solos in this section of the book should be played using the shuffle (or swing) rhythm (♫ = ♫) rather than even eighth notes.

Practice the next few solos in which the thumb plays a steady bass. Remember, the notes with the stems going down are to be played with the thumb, and the notes with the stems going up are to be played with the fingers.

The next blues fingerpicking solo use a steady bass in the thumb, but the fingers are a bit more complicated. Pay special attention to the triplets played with the first two fingers of the right hand. The slide should be from one fret below the written note.

Bob's Blues

CD #1
Track #31

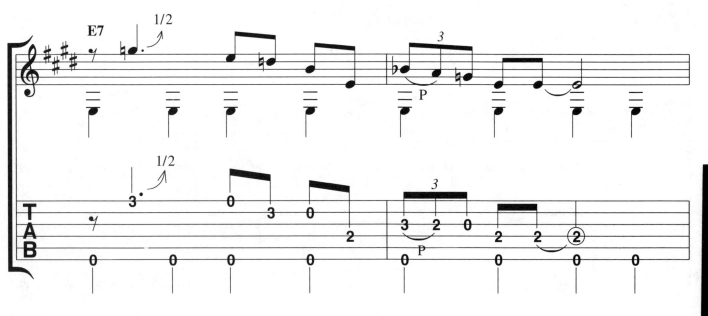

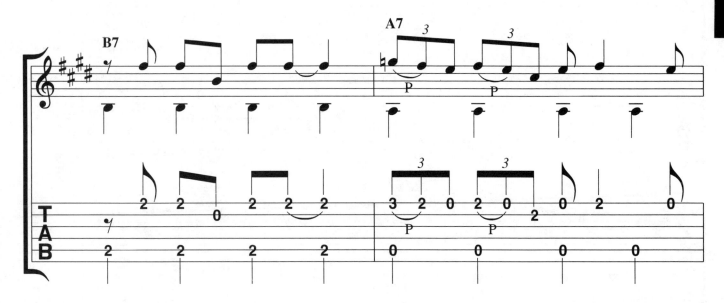

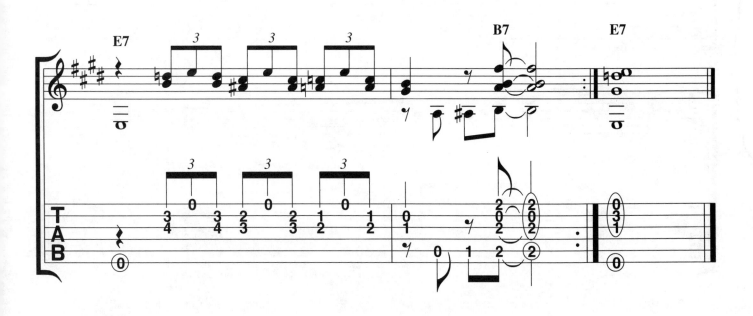

CD #1
Track #32

Late Night Blues

MC

In another type of fingerpicking solo, the thumb alternates between two strings while the fingers play the melody. This is sometimes referred to as the "alternating-bass" style. This technique is commonly used in playing ragtime solos.

The next exercise will get your thumb used to alternating between two strings. It is common in this style to hold the chord which is written above the measure. If a note that you are going to play is not in the chord, modify the fingering of the chord to enable you to get that note. Try to hold as much of the chord as possible.

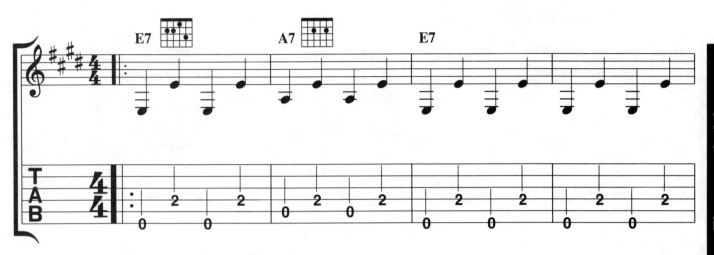

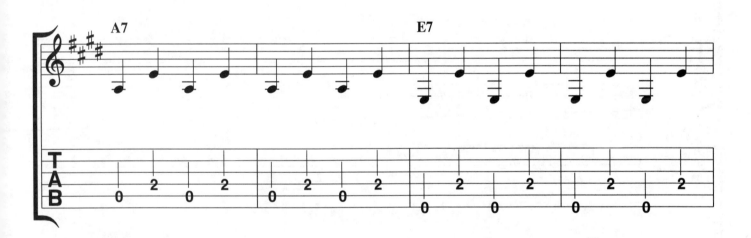

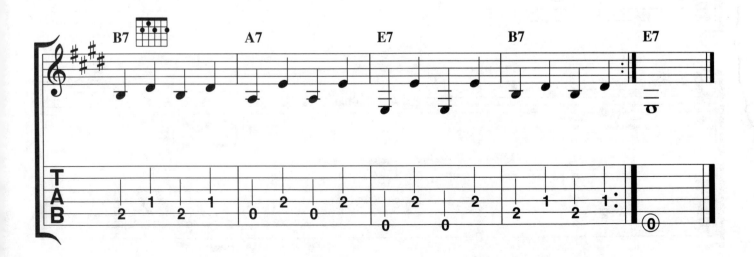

"Oscar's Blues" is a fingerpicking solo which uses the alternating-bass technique. Remember, while playing the notes in each measure, try to hold the chord written above the measure. The chord may have to be modified slightly by lifting a finger, or adding a finger, to play the written notes. Hold as much of the chord as possible.

CD #1
Track #33

Oscar's Blues

Fingerstyle Solo

MC

Fingerpicking Blues/Ragtime

When fingerpicking in a ragtime style, the technique is very similar to fingerpicking blues. Generally, a chord form may be held for one or more measures. The right-hand thumb usually alternates between two strings on the beat. In a ragtime style, the eighth notes are usually played with a swing rhythm.

The following two solos are in a fingerpicking ragtime style. The right-hand thumb alternates between two bass notes on the beat. Also, remember to play the eighth notes using swing rhythm.

CD #1
Track #34

June Rag

Fingerstyle Solo

♩ = 142 (♪♪ = ♪♪♪)

MC

Fingerpicking Blues/Ragtime

CD #1
Track #35

Ya Da Ya Da

Fingerstyle Solo

MC

Fingerpicking
Blues/Ragtime

Fingerpicking
Blues/Ragtime

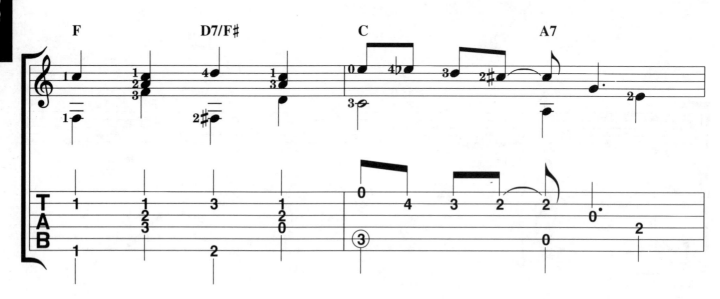

F#m Minor

In the key of F# minor we have three sharps — F#, C#, and G#. Thus, F# minor is "relative" to the key of A.

F#m Natural Minor Scale

Velocity Study #1

WB

Velocity Study #2

Key of F# Minor

F# Harmonic Minor

In the F# Harmonic Minor Scale, the 7th tone – E – is sharped. Remember, E sharp is played the same as F natural.

F# Harmonic Minor Scale

Velocity Study #1

WB

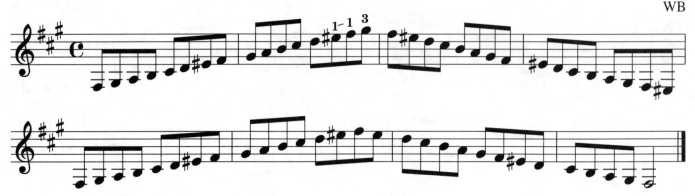

Velocity Study #2

Key of F# Minor

Lark in the Morning

Flatpick Solo
Freely, with expression   ♩ = 90

WB

The Unfortunate Rake

CD #1
Track #37
Flatpick Solo
Freely, with expression   ♩. = 88

WB

Key of F♯ Minor

CD #1
Track #38

Lost Roanoke

Flatpick Solo
Slowly, Lyrically

WB

CD #1
Track #39

The Black Sea

Flatpick Solo
Flowing tempo, expressive

WB

Key of F# Minor

Groove Time

Flatpick Solo
Swing feeling ♩ = 132

WB

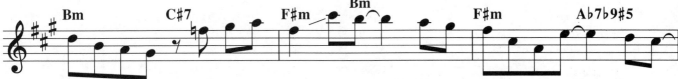

Norteñá

Flatpick Solo
Slowly, with expression

WB

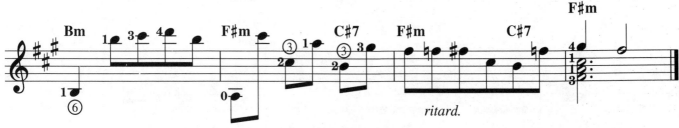

ritard.

Key of F♯ Minor

Hot Footin'

CD #1
Track #42

Flatpick Solo
Swing feeling ♩ = 138

WB

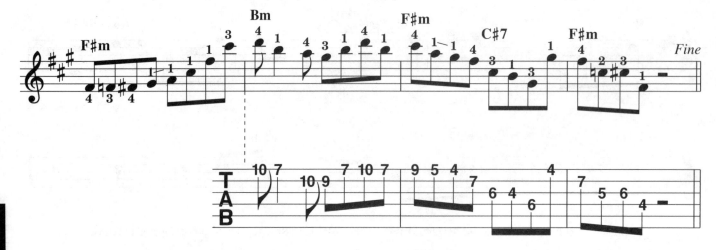

Key of F♯ Minor

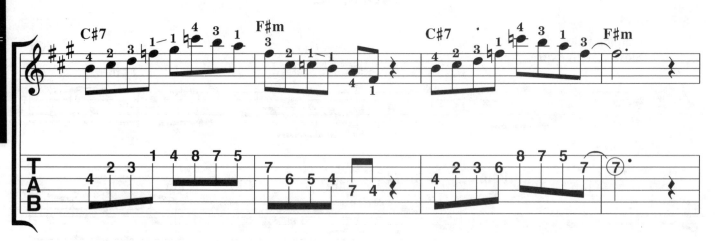

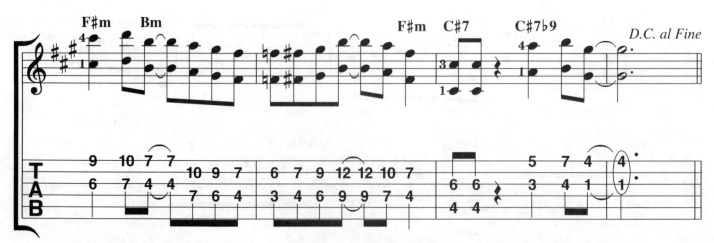

Allegretto

CD #1
Track #43

Flatpick Solo

WB
H. L. Clark

Allegretto ♩. = 68

Key of F♯ Minor

Key of F# Minor

CD #1
Track #44

Bistro

WB

Flatpick Solo
Swing feeling ♩ = 128

Key of F♯ Minor

Stinson Beach Rhumba

Fugue

Key of F# Minor

Basic Improvisation in F#m

Basic Chords and Arpeggios in F#m

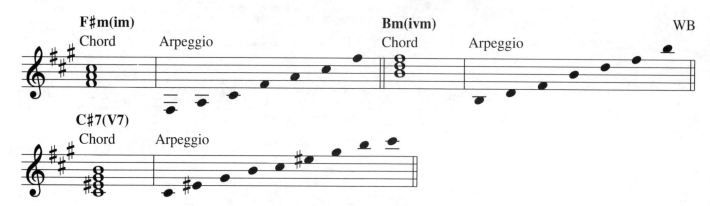

Basic Arpeggios

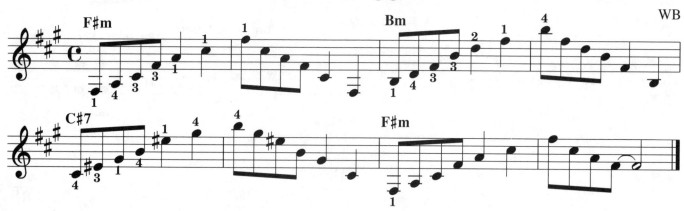

Passing Tone Study #1

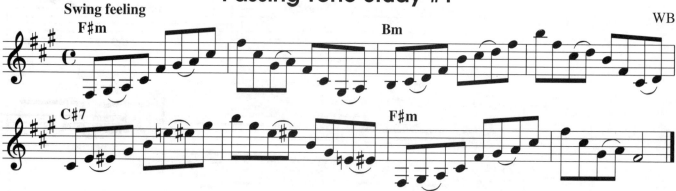

Passing Tone Study #2

Key of F# Minor

Passing Tone Study #3

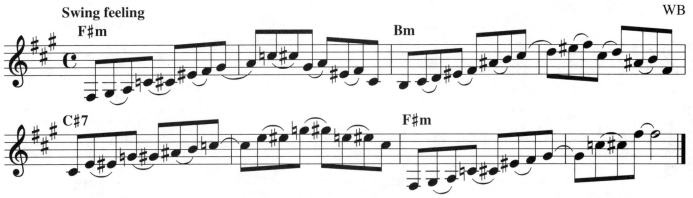

Rhythm Variation Study #1

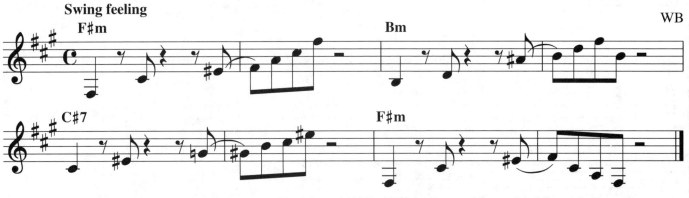

Rhythm Variation Study #2

Rhythm Variation Study #3

Key of F♯ Minor

Night Hawk

Fingerstyle or Flatpick Solo
Slowly ballad

CD #1
Track #49

WB

Key of F# Minor

Waltz for Wes

CD #1
Track #50

WB

Jazz waltz ♩ = 104

Key of F♯ Minor

CD #1
Track #51

Blue Dawn

Fingerstyle or Flatpick Solo
Slowly, with a beat

WB

Key of F♯ Minor

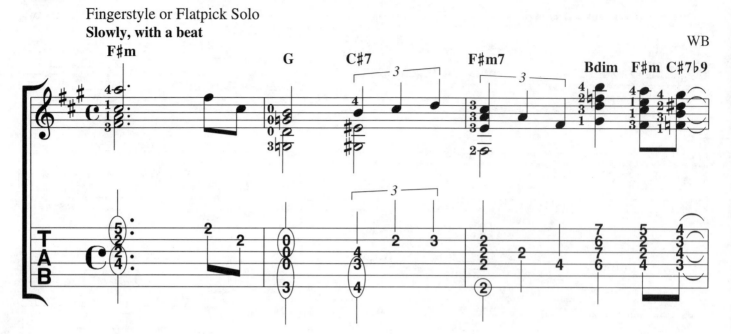

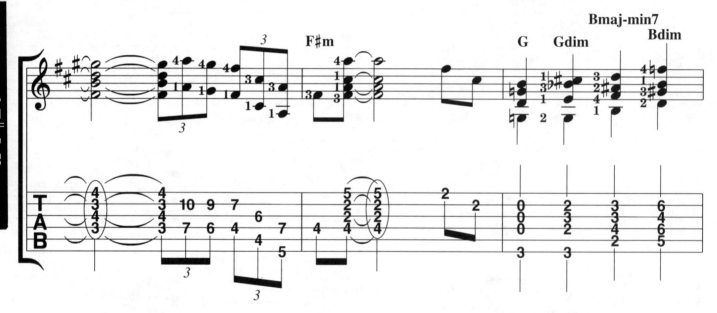

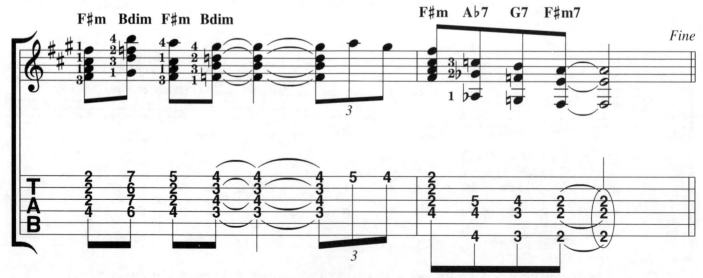

D.C. al Fine

Key of F# Minor

Quiet Moments

CD #1
Track #52

WB

Chords in the Key of F♯ Minor

i	ii	III	iv	V	VI	VII°
F♯m	G♯m7♭5	A	Bm	C♯7	D	E♯dim

Drawn below are the chords in the key of F♯ minor. The basic chords are shown first, followed by their embellishments and optional fingerings. The most commonly used chords in the key of F♯ minor are the i (F♯m), ii (G♯m7♭5), iv (Bm), and V (C♯7).
The chords A, D, and their embellishments are in the key of F♯ minor, but they are not drawn below because they have been presented earlier.

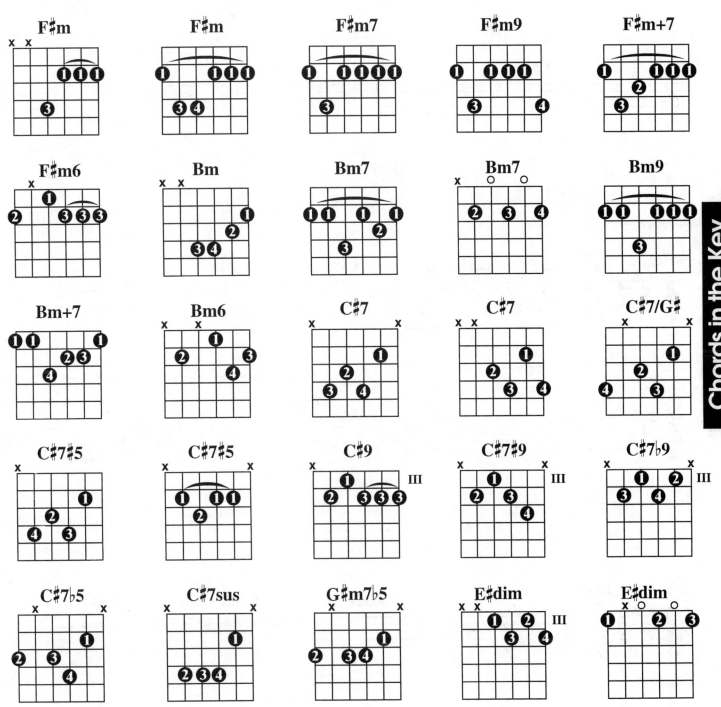

Chords Progressions in F♯ Minor

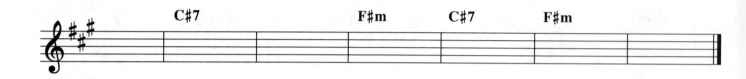

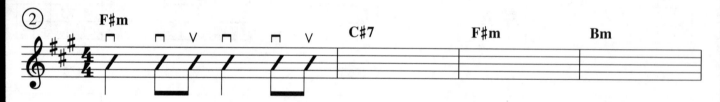

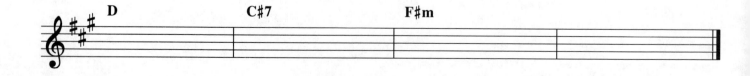

④
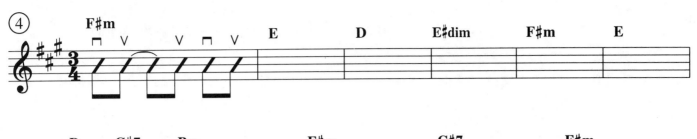

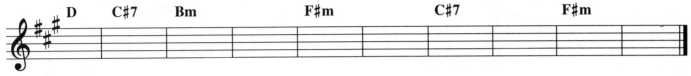

⑤
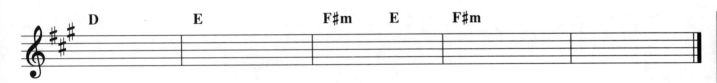

⑥
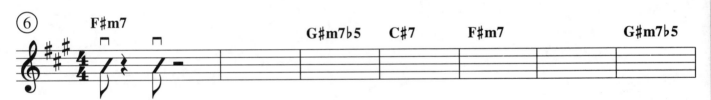

⑦

Chords in the Key of F# Minor

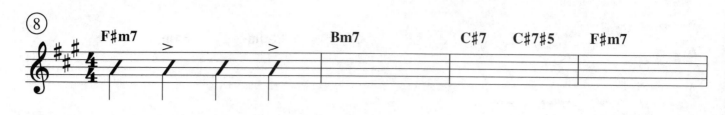

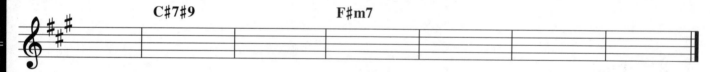

Blues Progression in F♯ Minor

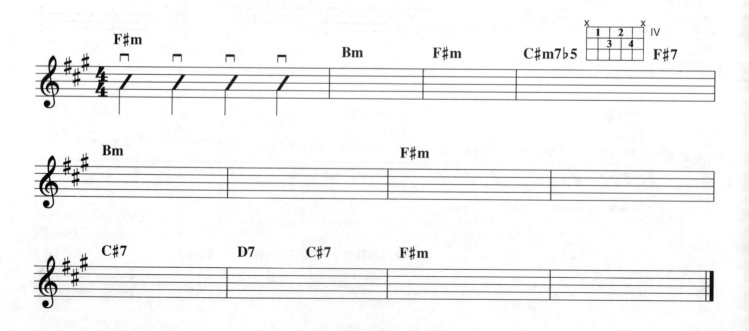

Blues in F♯ Minor

CD #1
Track #53

In the Pocket

MC

F# minor Scale Harmonized
(Harmonic Mode)

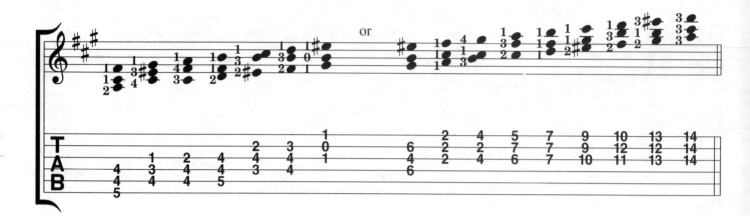

① **Swing feeling**   WB

② **Swing feeling**   WB

③ **Swing feeling**   WB

④   WB

F♯ Minor Etude

Fingerstyle Solo

♩ = 160

MC

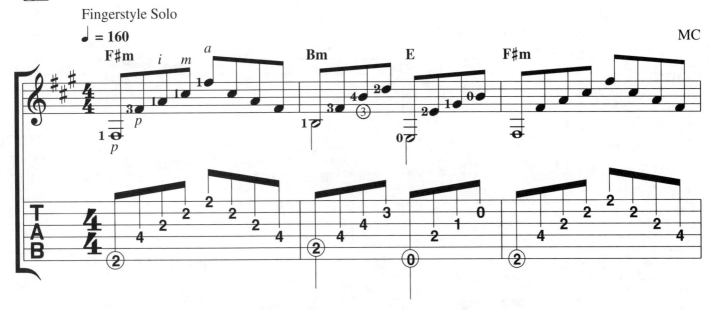

Fingerstyle Solos in F♯ Minor

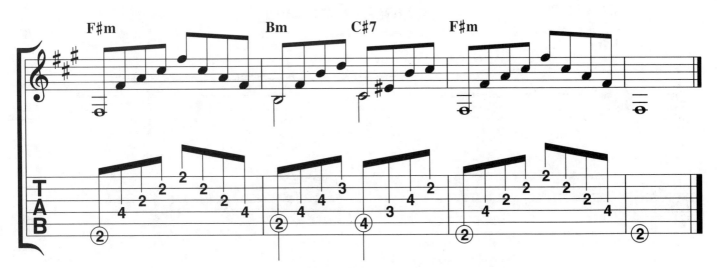

Left Alone

Spanish Dance

CD #1
Track #57

Forest Flowers

1st Guitar Pick or Fingerstyle
2nd Guitar Fingerstyle

WB
Finnish Folk Melody

Duet in F♯ Minor

Duet in F# Minor

Minor Pentatonic Improvisation

When improvising, solos are created instantly. Rather than simply showing which scale to use and writing, "Go for it," some guidelines and hints will be helpful in showing how to construct an improvised solo. The material in this section of the book will provide the tools necessary to give "training wheels" for improvisation. Suggestions for which notes, rhythms, and melodic ideas to use will be presented. Build original solos using the suggestions as a starting point. After catching on to the ideas, don't be afraid to experiment.

The scale used in the following exercises is the E minor pentatonic scale. This scale has been presented earlier, but for review, is drawn below. Practice the fingering.

E Minor Pentatonic

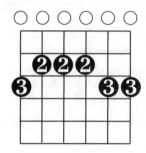

The improvised solos will be played over the chords to the twelve bar blues progression in the key of E. This progression is written below. Become familiar with these chord changes and the sound of the progression.

CD #1
Track #58

A concern of many guitarists learning to improvise is what rhythms to play. The following exercise will provide a "rhythm guide." In the exercise below, a part of the solo has been written in the every other measure. First practice the exercise playing only the notes which are written and counting (not playing) in the blank measures. Then, play the notes which are written, and in the blank measures, play any of the notes from the E minor pentatonic scale (any you would like) using the same rhythm which is written in the previous measure. When improvising to the twelve bar blues progression, any note from the minor pentatonic scale, which has the same letter name as the key, can be used. For example, when improvising to the blues in the key of E, any note from the E minor pentatonic scale can be used. Even when the chords change in the progression (A7 and B7 in blues in E), the notes from the E minor pentatonic scale can be used. Any of the notes from the scale will work, but some will sound better than others. This will be discussed later.

The solo will sound better if large skips are avoided. Play the exercise many times. Each time the exercise is played use different notes in the blank measures. At first, it may be helpful to write the improvised notes in the blank measures. Then, fill in the blanks with notes from the E minor pentatonic scale without writing them.

CD #1
Track #59

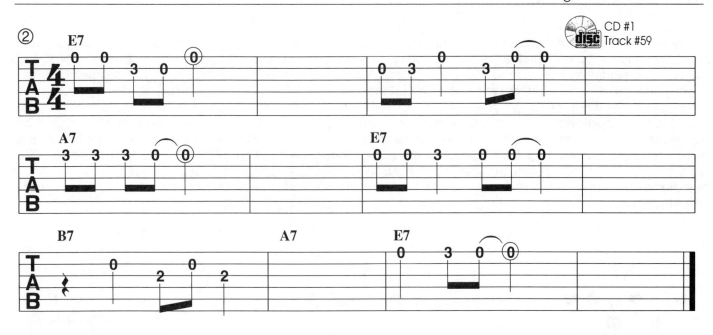

Another concern in improvising is which notes to use and in what order the notes of the scale can be played. Remember, when improvising over the twelve bar blues progression, any note from the E minor pentatonic scale can be used in the solo. The next exercise will present some ideas of what order to play the notes from the scale

In this exercise, play the notes which are written, and in the blank measures, use the same notes which were written in the previous measure but change the rhythm. Make sure there are four beats in each measure. The rhythms used in the blank measures are up to you, but the notes must be the same as in the previous measure.

CD #1
Track #60

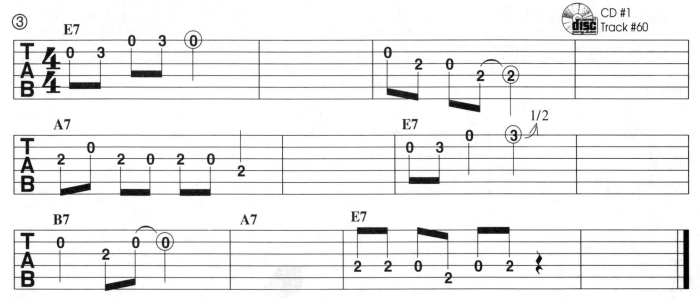

As was mentioned earlier in this section, some notes of the scale will sound better against certain chords. Generally, the notes which will sound the best are chord tones. A chord tone is a note which is contained in the chord being played for a particular measure. The guitar is a great instrument for finding chord tones. Without getting into a lengthy discussion on how chords are constructed, a simple way to find some chord tones is to look at the fingering of the chord. On the three diagrams below, the E minor pentatonic scale has been drawn using circles. The dots show the notes contained in the chord written above the diagram. Some of the notes in the chords will be in the fingering for the E minor pentatonic scale, and others may not. The fingerings for the chords may look a bit different (two notes on the same string). This is because there may be two fingerings for that chord in the first three frets. These are the notes from the scale which will sound the best when playing a solo over that particular chord. One of the best places in the measure to play a chord tone is on the first beat. The other beats can also be chord tones or other notes from the scale.

E7
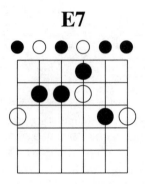

A7
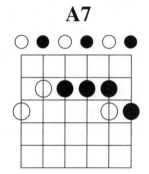

B7
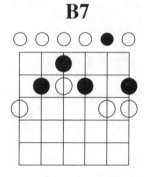

The following exercises will help in learning to use chord tones in building a solo. In the first exercise below, only one chord tone is played in a measure. Notice the note in the measure is a chord tone from the chord for that measure. After playing the exercise as written, play your own "one note solo" using different chord tones.

CD #1
Track #61

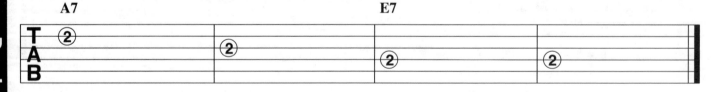

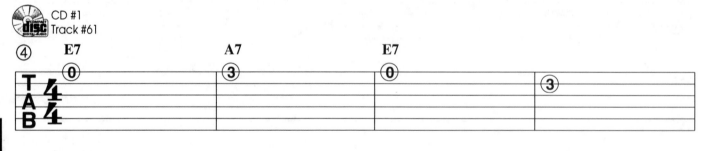

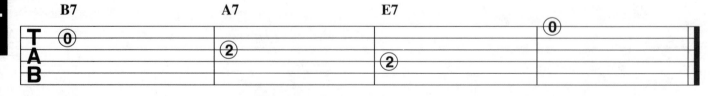

The next solo uses only two notes per measure, but they are still chord tones. Play this solo as written, then create your own "two note solo" using only chord tones.

CD #1
Track #62

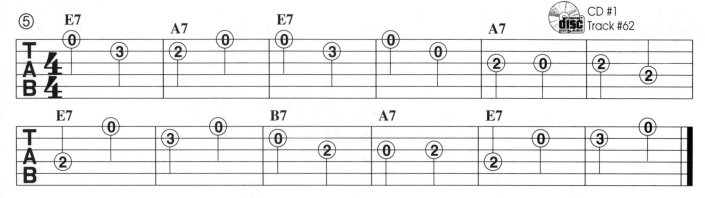

In the following solo, four notes are played in a measure. Chord tones have been used and so have other notes from the E minor pentatonic scale. Notice chord tones have been used on the first beat. After playing the solo as written, create an original "four note solo" using chord tones and notes from the scale.

CD #1
Track #63

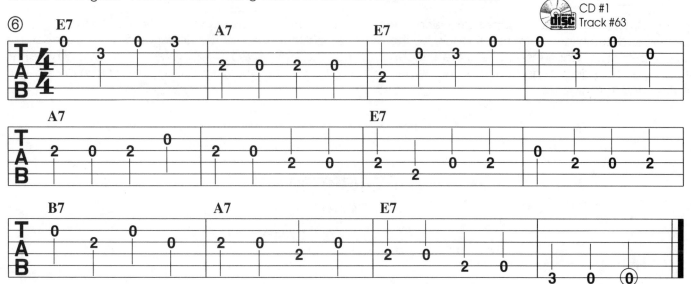

This next solo contains more than four notes in some of the measures. Notice the use of the E minor pentatonic scale and the frequent use of chord tones especially on the first beat of each measure. After playing this solo as written, create your own solo using more than four notes in some of the measures.

CD #1
Track #64

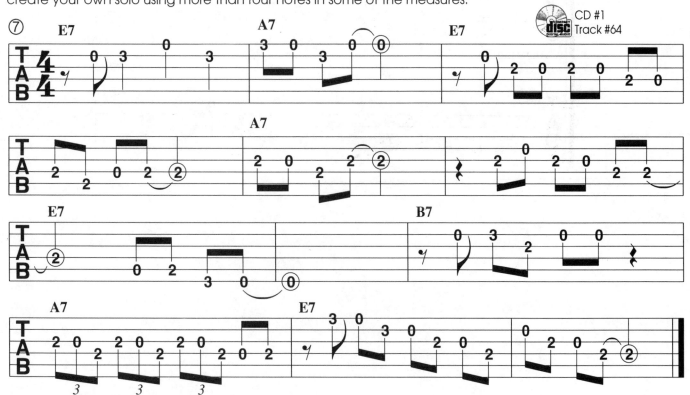

Minor Pentatonic Improvisation

Minor Pentatonic Extensions

The moveable minor pentatonic scales have been presented in book 2A of the "Mastering The Guitar" method. In this section of this book, extensions of the minor pentatonic scales and solos will be presented using those extensions. By means of a review, the minor pentatonic scale with it's root on the sixth string is shown below.

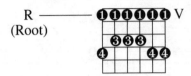

The diagram below shows the upper extension of the minor pentatonic scale with the root on the sixth string. If this scale were to begin in the fifth fret, it would be the A minor pentatonic scale. The upper extension of the scale is shown with circles. Fingerings can be altered depending upon the order of the notes played in the solo and whether the scale is ascending or descending. Shown below the diagram are the notes in this scale written in standard notation and in tablature.

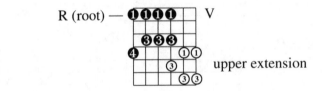

upper extension

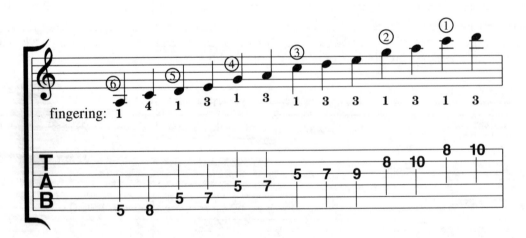

The following solo uses notes from the A minor pentatonic scale with the root in the sixth string and the upper extension.

The next diagram shows the lower extension of the minor pentatonic scale with the root in the sixth string. Practice the scale and the solo using the lower extension.

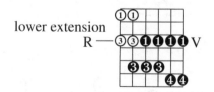

These are the notes if the root of the scale is in the 5th string. The scale is then A minor pentatonic.

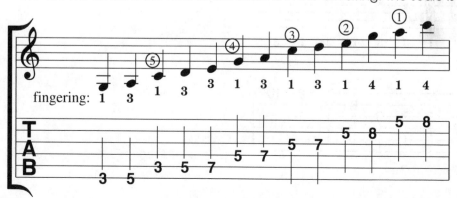

The following diagram shows the sixth-string-root minor pentatonic scale with the lower and upper extensions. Memorize this scale, and then practice the solo using the upper and lower extensions. Note the use of sequencing in the solo. When this scale begins in the 3rd fret, it is an A minor pentatonic scale. The root (R) would be in the sixth string, 5th fret (A).

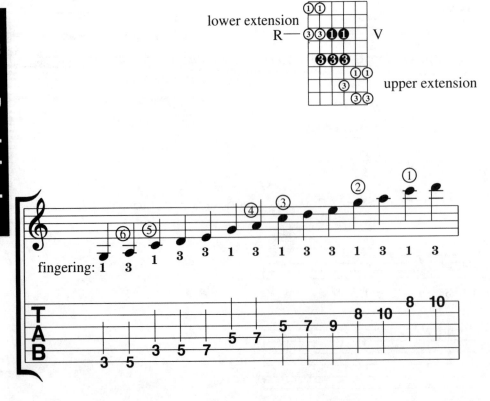

Comfort Zone

CD #1
Track #65   MC

The minor pentatonic scale with the root on the fifth string can also have lower and upper extensions. As a review, the basic minor pentatonic scale with the root on the fifth string is drawn below.

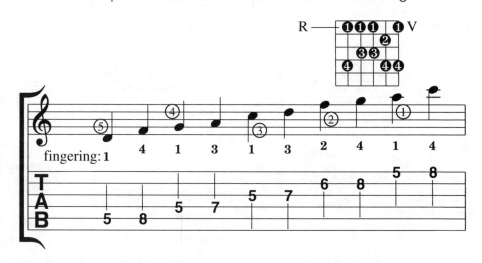

Minor Pentatonic Extensions

The next diagram shows the fifth-string-root minor pentatonic scale with an upper extension. Learn the scale and practice the solo using the extension. The scale below is the D minor pentatonic scale. The following solo also uses this scale.

The following diagram is the fifth-string-root minor pentatonic scale with a lower extension. Practice the scale and the solo using this minor pentatonic scale with the root on D.

In the next diagram, the minor pentatonic scale with the root on the fifth string is shown with the upper and lower extensions. Memorize the scale and practice the solo using the extensions.

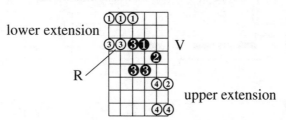

Written below are the notes of this scale when the root is on the fifth string, 5th fret (D). Practice this scale.

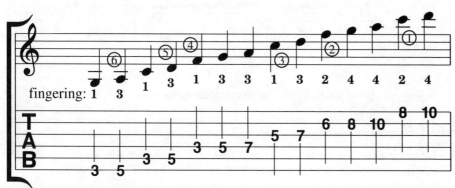

Minor Pentatonic Extensions

The following solo uses the upper and lower extensions of the D minor pentatonic scale.

Short and Sweet

CD #1
Track #66

Flatpick Solo

MC

Minor Pentatonic
Extensions

The following diagram illustrates how the minor pentatonic scales with roots on the sixth string and the root on the fifth string can merge. This makes it possible to cover the entire neck no matter which key you're in. The white and black fingering shows the separate scales with their extensions. Memorize this scale.

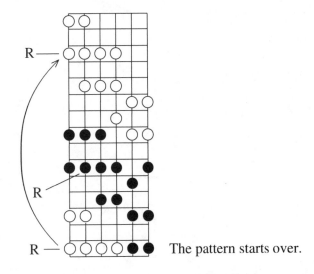

The pattern starts over.

Practice the next solo, which uses the combining of the G minor pentatonic scales. The roots are on G. Then practice improvising your own solos connecting these scales.

Key of E♭

In the key of E♭ we have three flats — B♭, E♭, and A♭.

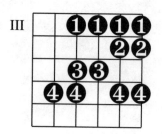

Velocity Study #1

Velocity Study #2

Velocity Study #3

E♭ Scale / Extended Range

Velocity Study #4

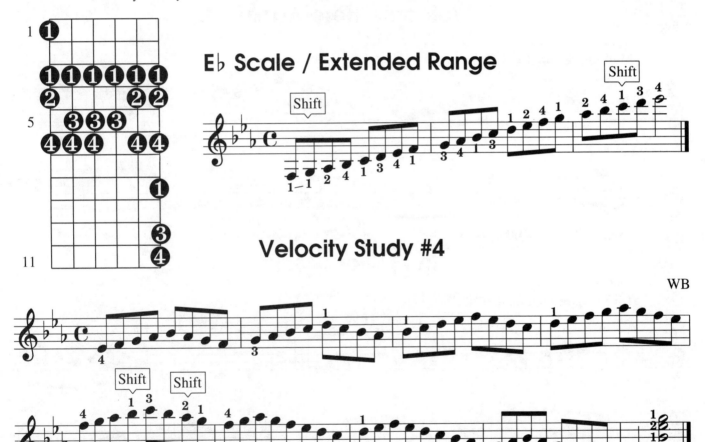

Extended Range Etude

Key of E♭

CD #1
Track #68

Richard's Reel

Flatpick

Moderately ♩ = 100

WB

CD #1
Track #69

Welcome Here Again

Flatpick

WB

Medium tempo ♩ = 70

CD #1
Track #70

The Miller's Maid

Flatpick

Lively, dance tempo ♩ = 70

WB

Key of E♭

Hell Among the Yearlings

CD #1
Track #71

Flatpick Solo
Lively tempo ♩ = 152

WB
Fiddle Tune

Wind that Shakes the Barley

CD #1
Track #72

Flatpick Solo
With a solid beat ♩ = 80

WB
Fiddle Tune

Key of E♭

CD #1
Track #73

Little House Round the Corner

Flatpick Solo

Medium jig tempo ♩. = 84

WB

CD #1
Track #74

Jackson's Jig

Flatpick Solo

Flowing tempo ♩. = 88

WB

Key of E♭

Off She Goes

Flatpick Solo
Moderately ♩. = 100

WB

Kerry Dance

Flatpick Solo
Medium tempo ♩. = 88

WB

Come Again?

Flatpick Solo
♩. = 90

WB

Key of E♭

The Gates of Limerick

The Dancing Brat

Crazy Jake

Key of Eb

Key of E♭

Study

CD #2
Track #1

Kreutzer

Flatpick Solo

Andante ♩ = 94

Cruisin

CD #2
Track #2

WB

Ee's Flat

CD #2
Track #3

WB

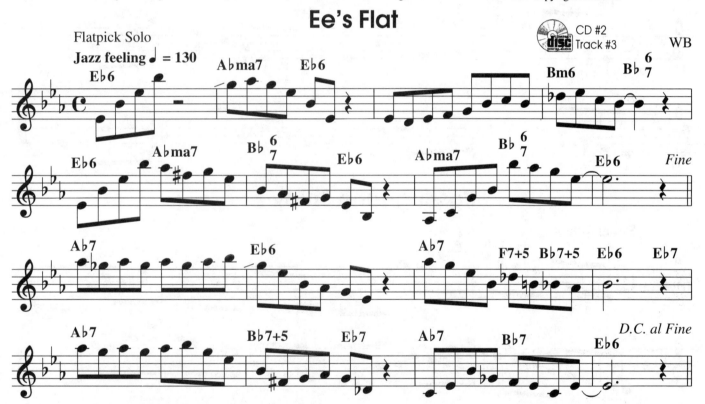

Cabin Fever

CD #2
Track #4

WB

Key of E♭

Basic Improvisation in E♭

Basic Chords and Arpeggios in E♭

Basic Arpeggios

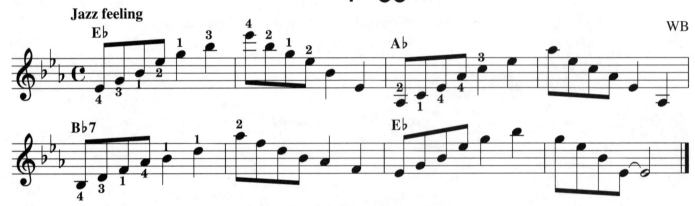

Passing Tone Study #1

Passing Tone Study #2

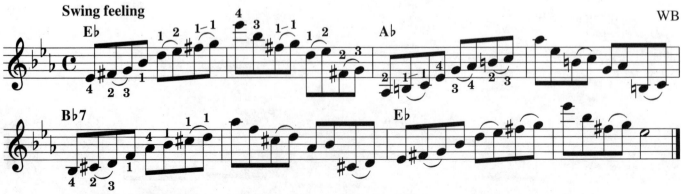

Chords/Arpeggios

Passing Tone Study #3

Rhythmic Variation Study #1

Rhythmic Variation Study #2

Rhythmic Variation Study #3

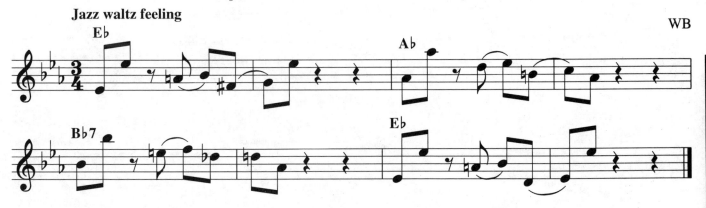

Chords/Arpeggios

CD #2
Track #5

Back at the Woodshed

Flatpick Solo
Moderately ♩ = 76

WB

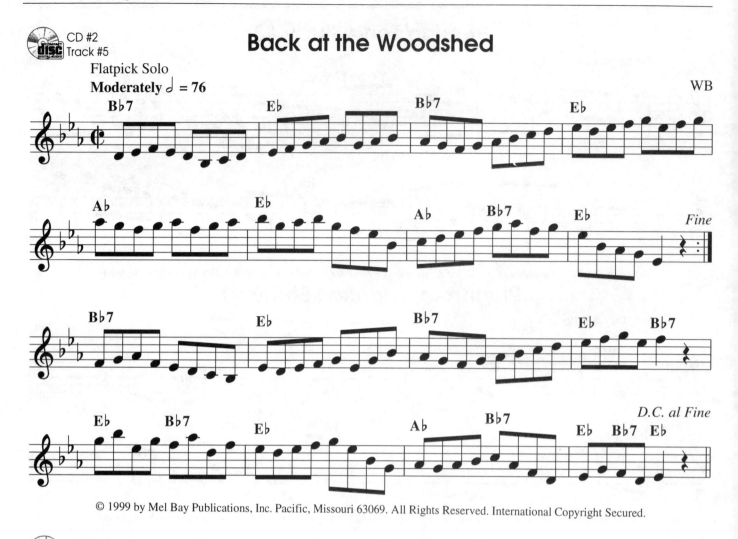

CD #2
Track #6

Slim Pickings

Flatpick Solo
♩ = 72

WB

Key of E♭

E♭ Major Scale Harmonized
(Triads)

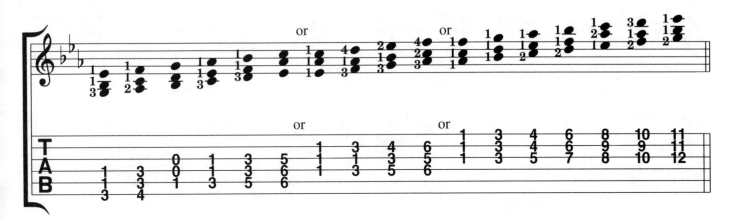

E♭ Major Scale Harmonized

For Kari

CD #2
Track #7

MC

Fingerstyle Solo

Fingerstyle
Solos in E♭

Adagio

CD #2
Track #8

Fingerstyle Solo

MC

Fingerstyle
Solos in E♭

CD #2
Track #9

Modenga

Fingerstyle Solos in E♭

Free Flight

CD #2
Track #10

WB

Spring Serenade

CD #2
Track #11

WB

+ = Thumb

Fingerstyle Solos in Eb

CD #2
Track #12

Gentle Bossa

Fingerstyle Solo

MC

Valse

Fingerstyle Solo

MC

Fingerstyle Solos in E♭

Fingerstyle or Flatpick Solo
Slow, ballad

Star Eyes

CD #2
Track #14

WB

* To play this note — while holding the chord, press down the high D with the right hand index finger and pluck the string with your right hand thumb.

Chords in the Key of E♭

I	ii	iii	IV	V	vi	VII°
E♭	Fm	Gm	A♭	B♭7	Cm	Ddim

Drawn below are the chords in the key of E♭. The basic chords are shown first, followed by their embellishments and optional fingerings.

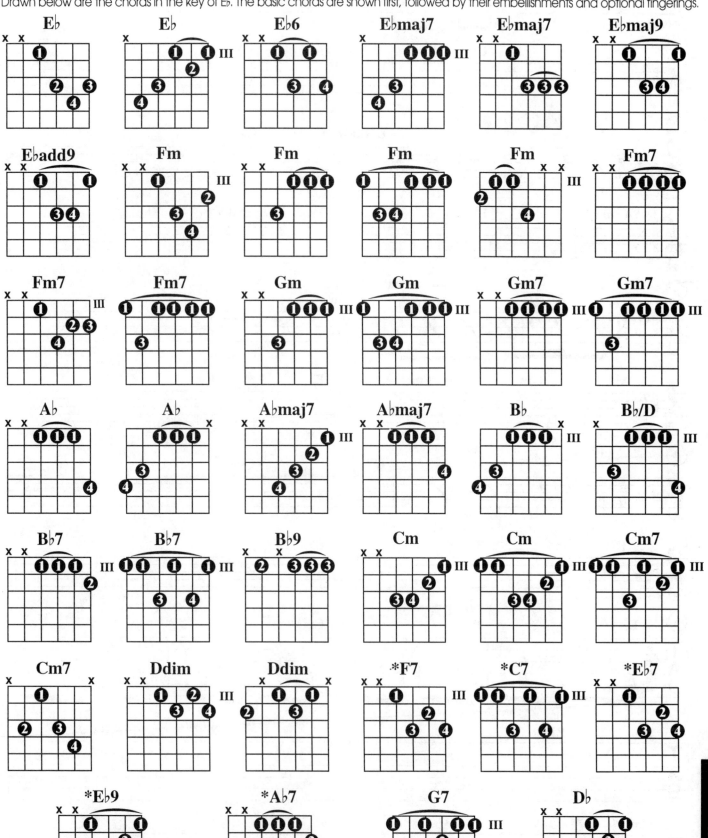

* These chords are not in the key of E♭. However, they are frequently used in that key.

Chord Progressions in the Key of E Flat

Licks, Fills, and Breaks in the Key of E♭

Written below are many licks, fills, and breaks which can be used in the key of A. When combined with scales, they can add color and credibility to an improvised solo.

The following solo contains licks, fills, and breaks in the key of E♭, so they can be easily seen. The licks, fills, and breaks have been boxed.

In a Straight Line

Blues in the Key of E Flat

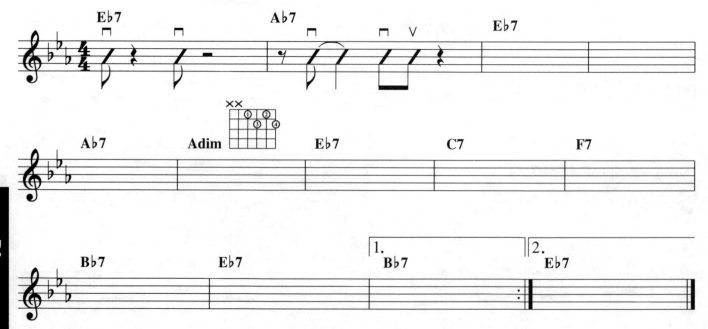

Shades of Blues

CD #2
Track #16

MC

Blues in the
Key of E♭

Gavotte

CD #2
Track #17

WB
J. S. Bach

Flatpick Solo

Allegro ♩ = 104

Duets in E♭

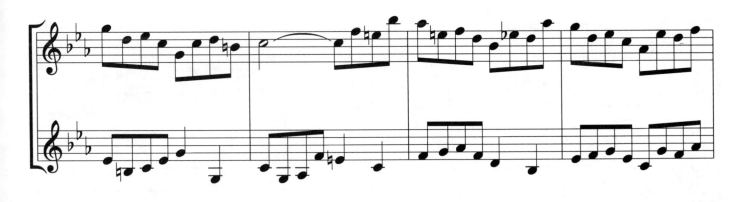

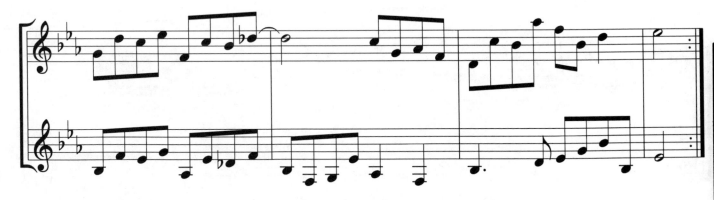

Duets in E♭

CD #2
Track #18

Sleeper's Wake

1st Part Flatpick or Fingerstyle
2nd Part Fingerstyle

WB
J. S. Bach

Larghetto ♩ = 58

Duets in E♭

Duets in E♭

13th Fret

13th Fret

Duets in E♭

Barre Notation

The letter C written above music for guitar indicates a finger (usually the left hand index finger) is to be barred across all six strings to play the notes or chord which appear under the C. When all the strings are barred, this is sometimes referred to as a full bar. A Roman numeral indicates the fret in which the bar finger is placed. If a broken line extends to the right of the C, this indicates the barre finger is to be held down until the broken line stops.

If 1/2C, or ₵ is written, this indicates to bar 1/2 of the strings (strings one, two, and three). If 2/3 is written, bar four of the six strings. The chart below shows the symbols for barring and how they are used. This type of notation is used as a aid to the player in locating portions of the music where a bar is used. This notation is generally used in music for fingerstyle guitar.

C	bar all six strings
1/2 C or ₵	bar half the strings (strings one, two, and three)
2/3 C	bar strings 1-4
1/3 C	bar strings one and two
5/6 C	bar strings 1-5

The following solo contains some partial bars.

Nikki's Waltz

CD #2 Track #19   MC

Barre Notation

The next three solos contain partial and full bars.

Lament

Fingerstyle Solo
♩ = 66

CD #2
Track #20

MC

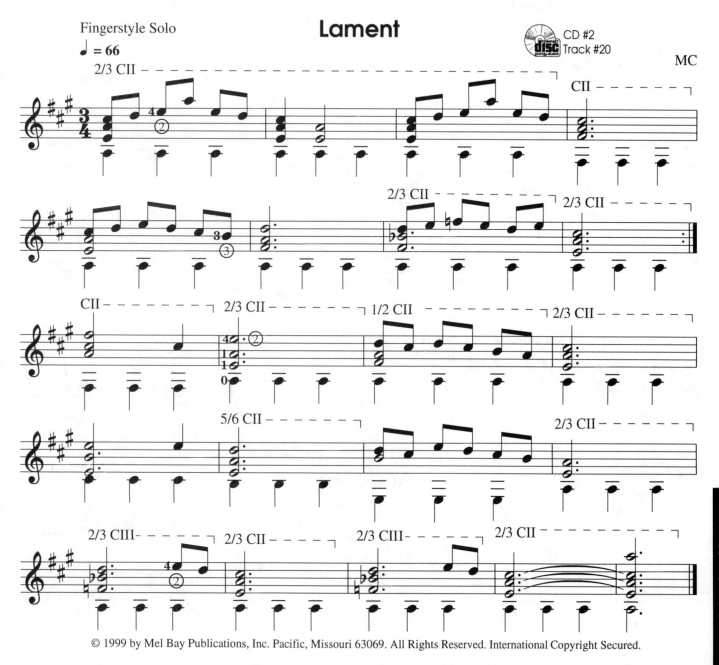

Barre Notation

The "Sarabanda" by Ronalli contains partial bars, and in measure six, the full bar is used.

indicates to strum down with the thumb

strum up with the index finger

Dot Com

Flatpick Solo

Barre Notation

Key of C Minor

The key of C minor has three flats — Bb, Eb, and Ab.

The Natural C Minor Scale

Velocity Study

The C Harmonic Minor Scale

Velocity Study

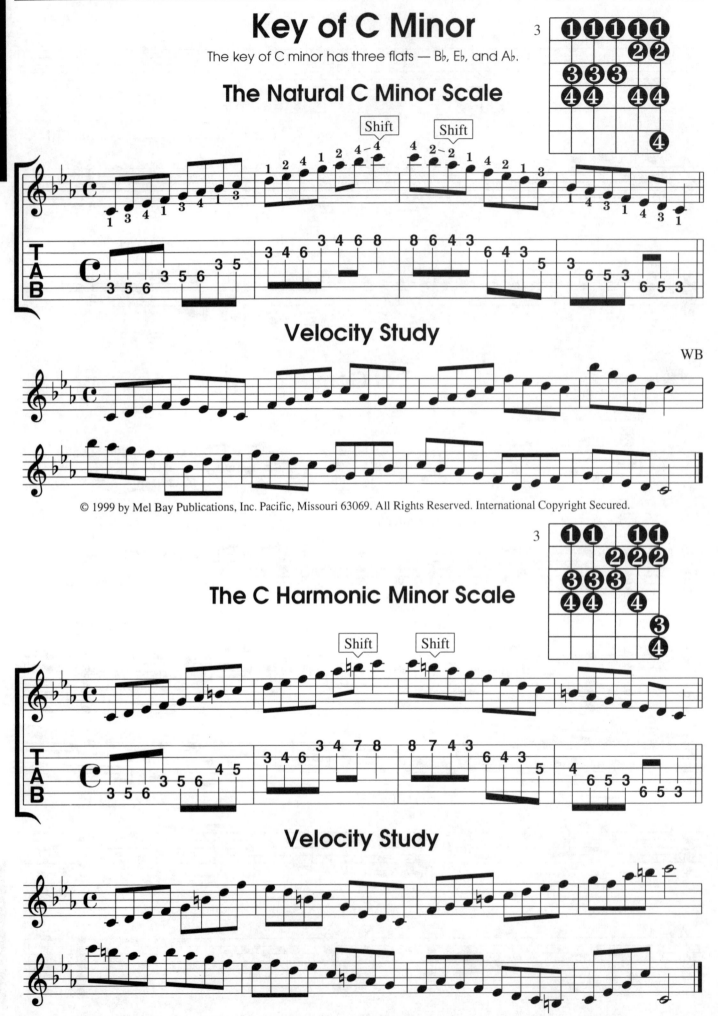

Steppe

Flatpick Solo

Andante ♩ = 68

CD #2
Track #24

WB

Molambe

Flatpick Solo

Salsa ♩ = 128

CD #2
Track #25

WB

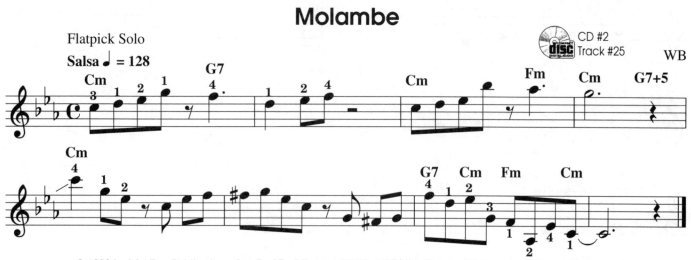

Singular Invention

Flatpick Solo

Moderately ♩. = 80

CD #2
Track #26

WB

Key of C Minor

CD #2
Track #27

Vyaltsevo

Flatpick Solo

Flowing tempo ♩ = 164

WB

CD #2
Track #28

Gypsy Dance

Flatpick Solo

With solid rhythm ♩ = 132

WB

Revival Blues

Flatpick Solo

WB

Minor Detail

Flatpick Solo

WB

Key of C Minor

Agitato

CD #2
Track #31

Flatpick Solo
Slowly, with expression ♩ = 60

WB

Funky Mr. Green

Walkin'

For Wes

CD #2
Track #34

WB

Flatpick Solo
Moderately, jazz feeling ♩ = 144

High Steppin'

CD #2
Track #35

WB

Flatpick Solo
Fast, jazz tempo ♩ = 152

CD #2
Track #36

Slick Pickin'

Flatpick Solo
Medium jazz ♩ = 148

WB

CD #2
Track #37

Vanguard

Flatpick Solo
Easy jazz tempo ♩ = 144

WB

Key of C Minor

CD #2
Track #38

Reel Jazz

Flatpick Solo

Lively tempo ♩ = 156

WB

CD #2
Track #39

Jazz Etude

Flatpick Solo

Medium, jazz tempo ♩ = 140

WB

CD #2
Track #40

Cm Study

Flatpick Solo

WB

© 1999 by Mel Bay Publications, Inc. Pacific, Missouri 63069. All Rights Reserved. International Copyright Secured.

CD #2
Track #41

Valse

Flatpick Solo

WB

© 1999 by Mel Bay Publications, Inc. Pacific, Missouri 63069. All Rights Reserved. International Copyright Secured.

Key of C Minor

Makin' Time

CD #2
Track #42

MC

CD #2
Track #43

Easy Flow

Flatpick Solo

♩ = 76

Cm

MC

G7